Teacher's Manual

# IDIOMS
## for
## Everyday Use

The Basic Text for
Learning and Communicating
with English Idioms

**Milada Broukal**

National Textbook Company
**NTC** a division of *NTC Publishing Group* • Lincolnwood, Illinois USA

**1995 Printing**

Published by National Textbook Company, a division of NTC Publishing Group.
©1994 by NTC Publishing Group, 4255 West Touhy Avenue,
Lincolnwood (Chicago), Illinois 60646-1975 U.S.A.
Manufactured in the United States of America.

5 6 7 8 9 0 VP 9 8 7 6 5 4 3 2

# Contents

# Introduction

## OVERVIEW OF *IDIOMS FOR EVERYDAY USE*

*Idioms for Everyday Use* is a text that presents over 200 of the most commonly used American idioms. It is appropriate for use by high beginning and intermediate level students of English. Learners are introduced to the idioms in context, study their meanings, and practice them in a variety of activities. After working in the text, students should both understand the idioms and feel confident about using them in their own conversations.

Since idioms can be both difficult and confusing for students of English, ways of facilitating learning them is important. As in most learning, associations help students to recall material. To facilitate associations, the idioms have been organized into twenty units, each with a simple "theme": for example, idioms with color words, idioms with clothes words, idioms with plant words, and so on. This thematic focus should help students recall the idioms. Also, the number of idioms in each unit has been limited to eleven to make recall easier.

## The Organization of the Text

Each of the twenty units in the text has these parts:

1. **Reading**

   This is a story containing some of the idioms in the unit. It provides the students with their first exposure to the idioms. Each story is accompanied by a cartoon and is followed by questions. The material in this Teacher's Manual provides prereading questions to help students understand the content of the reading, as well as postreading comprehension questions and activities.

2. **Meanings**

   This part helps students actively determine the meanings of the idioms. It contains an example showing each idiom in context. Following the examples are simple definitions of the idioms. The students' task is to match the context sentences with the definitions.

3. **Practice**

   This part gives students a chance to practice using the idioms in several contexts. There are two exercises in **Practice**. In the first exercise, students check whether they correctly understand the meaning of the idiom. Students are presented with a context and then asked whether a certain idiom fits the context. The second exercise varies in type. Often students are asked to find an error in the form of the idiom. In other cases, they are asked to complete a sentence with the appropriate idiom.

4. **Conversation**

   This part allows for further practice of idioms in the context of natural-sounding dialogues, which students can act out as mini role-plays. As a follow-up, in a section called **On Your Own,** students work in pairs to create their own role-plays incorporating the idioms.

5. **Discussion**

   In this part, students discuss topics related to the idioms in the unit. Typically students are asked if they know other English idioms related to the theme of the unit (for example, other idioms with color words) or if there are similar idioms in their own language. Often students are asked to provide real-life stories or examples that illustrate one of the idioms.

   Finally, the text contains five review units and a glossary. The glossary lists the idioms in alphabetical order and gives their definitions. It also gives the number of the unit where the idiom is covered. Students can use the list for help as they work in the book or for reference once they have finished work in the text.

## About This Teacher's Manual

This Teacher's Manual has three parts:

1. **Introduction**

   This introduction explains the purpose and design of the text and provides suggestions for using it in the classroom.

2. **Presenting the Units**

   This part contains suggestions for presenting the text, unit by unit. (a) First, there is an activity to introduce the theme of the unit to the students and to help them with basic vocabulary relating to the unit theme. (b) Next, there is material for presenting the reading that opens each unit (prereading questions, comprehensive questions, test your memory of the idioms). (c) Finally, there are several suggested follow-up activities for students to do once they have completed the unit. Which, if any of these activities, to use will depend both on time and the level of the class.

3. **Answer Key**

   This part contains answers for the activities in the student text. Answers are included for the parts titled **Meanings** and **Practice** and for the **Review Units.**

## SUGGESTIONS FOR USING THE TEXT

The material in the text and Teacher's Manual is flexible so that it can be used in a variety of ways. Most of the material is suited for students working in pairs and in small groups.

One possibility is to introduce each unit as a class activity, using the material in **Presenting the Units** in this Teacher's Manual both to preview the unit theme and to work with the unit reading.

The exercises in the text, **Meanings** and **Practice,** can be done by students in pairs, in small groups, or independently. The **Conversation** part is, of course, best done as a pair activity, although you could read through the dialogues as a class activity first to check comprehension and have the class or group produce some sample dialogues as models. Finally, **Discussion** is to be done in small groups or with the whole class.

You could then use one of the **Follow-up** activities in this Teacher's Manual to have students review the idioms in the unit or extend their knowledge of idioms

# Unit 1
# Idioms from Colors

## INTRODUCTION

Tell students that they are going to learn idioms with color words. Ask them this:

How many colors do you know in English? Name them and write them down.

## PRESENTATION OF THE READING
### Prereading Questions

Have students discuss these questions before they read the story:

1. Do you have an account in a bank?
2. Do you have a checking account? What does a checking account let you do?
3. What happens when you have no money in your checking account and you write a check?
4. Do banks sometimes make mistakes?

## COMPREHENSION QUESTIONS

Have students answer these questions after they read the story:

1. What did the person get from the bank?

   (The person got a letter from the bank.)
2. Was the person expecting a letter from the bank?

   (No. The person wasn't expecting the letter. It came out of the blue.)
3. Did the letter say that the person had extra money in the bank?

   (No, the letter said that the person had no money in the bank. The letter said that the person was in the red.)
4. Who made the mistake?

   (The bank made the mistake.)
5. What did the manager do?

   (The manager reopened the account immediately. The manager cut through all the red tape.)
6. Could the person write checks again?

   (Yes, the person could. The person had the green light to write checks.)

## Test Your Memory of the Idioms

Have students do this activity:

How many colors were there in the idioms in the story? Write down as many colors as you can remember. Then write down as many of the idioms with colors as you can.

## FOLLOW-UP

After students have completed the activities in the unit, have them do one or both of these activities:

1. There are many idioms in English with colors. Here are some others you might want to introduce to the students. You may want students to look in dictionaries and other reference books to find others to add to the list. Help students to write sentences using the idioms.

   to black out: to faint, lose consciousness

   to give someone a black eye: to hit someone so that a dark mark appears around the person's eye; to hurt a person's reputation

   to have a green thumb: to have the ability to grow plants well

   to catch someone red-handed: to catch someone doing something wrong

   to see red: to get angry

   with flying colors: easily and excellently

2. Write down the eleven idioms in the unit on the board, eliminating the color words. Have students supply the color words.

# Unit 2
# Idioms from Food

## INTRODUCTION

Tell students that they are going to learn idioms with names of food. Ask them these questions:

Do you know what these foods are?

a lemon    nuts    a cake    bananas    a peach

Which are fruits?

What kind of food is baloney? (Explain that it is a kind of sausage. It is also called "bologna."

What is a pickle? (Explain that it is a cucumber in salt water with vinegar. Foods that are put in salt water with vinegar are called "pickled." Ask students what kinds of foods can be pickled.)

## PRESENTATION OF THE READING

### Prereading Questions

Have students discuss these questions before they read the story:

1. Is it a good idea to buy a used car?
2. How can you tell if a car works well?
3. What kinds or makes of American cars do you know? Name them.
4. If someone sues you, what happens?

## COMPREHENSION QUESTIONS

Have students answer these questions after they read the story:

1. For how much did the person buy the car?
   (The person bought the car for $300.)
2. Did the engine of the car start?
   (Yes, it did. Starting the engine was a piece of cake. There was no problem.)
3. What was wrong with the car?
   (The brakes didn't work. The car was a lemon.)

4. What kind of car did the person hit?

   (The person hit a Cadillac.)

5. What did the owner of the Cadillac do?

   (He went bananas and sued the person.)

6. What must the person do for the owner of the Cadillac?

   (The person has to pay the owner of the Cadillac $2,000.)

7. What happened to the car?

   (The person's friend took it to the garbage dump.)

## Test Your Memory of the Idioms

Have students do this activity:

How many food words were there in the idioms in the story? Write down as many foods as you can remember. Then write down as many of the idioms with food as you can.

## FOLLOW-UP

After students have completed the activities in the unit, have them do one or both of these activities:

1. Here are some other idioms with foods you might want to introduce to the students.

   bread and butter: one's livelihood, income

   to butter someone up: to flatter someone, often insincerely

   as cool as a cucumber: very calm, never upset

   the cream of the crop: the very best in the group

   to lay an egg: to give a bad performance

   to put all one's eggs in one basket: to risk everything on one thing

   to spill the beans: to tell a secret

   food for thought: something to think about

2. On the board, write down the definitions from the Meanings section in the text. Have students write the idiom for each definition.

# Unit 3
# Idioms from Numbers

## INTRODUCTION

Tell students that they are going to learn idioms with numbers in them. Have them do these activities:

What number can you count to in English?
Count in ordinal numbers from one to twenty. (first, second, third, . . .)
How many are in a dozen? What things are sold in dozens? (eggs)

## PRESENTATION OF THE READING

### Prereading Questions

Have students discuss these questions before they read the story:

1. Have you ever gone fishing? Do you like fishing?
2. Where can you go to catch fish?
3. What do you need to catch a fish?

### Comprehension Questions

Have students answer these questions after they read the story:

1. Does the person have a clear opinion on fishing?
   (No. The person does not have a clear opinion. The person is of two minds about it.)
2. What does the person think at first sight?
   (The person thinks that fishing is fun.)
3. How does the person feel about fishing after thinking about it?
   (The person doesn't like to handle a fish after it is caught.)
4. What can people who like fishing do?
   (They can look at a river or a lake and know where the fish are.)
5. How do they do this?
   (They have a sixth sense.)
6. Do you think that the person telling the story is good at fishing?
   (No.)

## Test Your Memory of the Idioms

Have students do this activity:

> How many idioms with numbers were there in the story? Write down as many of the idioms with numbers as you can remember.

# FOLLOW-UP

After students have completed the activities in the unit, have them do one or both of these activities:

1. Write the eleven idioms in the unit on the board, eliminating the number words. Have students supply the number words.
2. Write sentences like the following on the board. Have students replace the underlined words with the idioms. Check that students use the correct forms.

   a. I was tired and I took <u>a short nap</u> this afternoon.

   b. I was <u>very happy</u> when I got a new job.

   c. That TV program is <u>the very best</u>.

   d. I <u>couldn't decide</u> whether to stay home or go out.

   e. <u>After a quick look</u>, I thought the job would be easy.

   f. My friend has <u>a special understanding and feeling</u> for when it is going to rain.

   g. I <u>finally came to a conclusion</u> and decided that my friends were giving me a surprise party.

# Unit 4
# Idioms from Parts of the Body

## INTRODUCTION

Tell students that they are going to learn idioms with parts of the body. Ask them this question:

Name the parts of the body that you know. List as many as you can.

## PRESENTATION OF THE READING
### Prereading Questions

Have students discuss these questions before they read the story:

1. Have you studied English in school before? Did you get to know people in your class? What kinds of people were in your class?
2. Has anyone ever played a joke on you and made you believe something that was not true?

## COMPREHENSION QUESTIONS

Have students answer these questions after they read the story:

1. What kinds of people were in the English class?
   (There were unusual people.)
2. What did one student learn by heart?
   (The student learned all the idioms in the book.)
3. What did the student who had a sweet tooth like?
   (The student liked sweets like cake and breads.)
4. What happened to two other students?
   (They fell head over heels in love.)
5. One student was always pulling someone's leg. What joke did he play?
   (He made the other students think that the teacher had given a long assignment.)
6. How did the students feel about the long assignment?
   (They had long faces. They had unhappy expressions on their faces.)

## Test Your Memory of the Idioms

Have students do this activity:

> How many parts of the body were there in the idioms in the story? Write down as many of them as you can remember. Then write down as many of the idioms with parts of the body as you can.

# FOLLOW-UP

After students have completed the activities in the unit, have them do one or both of these activities:

1. There are many idioms in English with parts of the body. Here are some others you might want to introduce to the students. You may want students to look in dictionaries and other reference books to find others to add to the list. Help students to write sentences with the idioms.

    to button one's lip: to keep quiet

    to toe the mark: to follow the rules

    to talk one's head off: to talk a lot

    to get to the heart of the matter: to talk about the most important point

    to lose heart: to become discouraged

    to put one's foot in one's mouth: to say something stupid

2. On the board, write down the definitions from the Meanings section in the text. Have students write the idiom for each definition.

# Unit 5
# Idioms from People

## INTRODUCTION

Tell students that they are going to learn idioms with people and people's names. Do these activities:

Let's look at some common English names for people.

Here are some last names, or family names:

Jones    Robinson    McCoy

Do you know any others?

Here are some typical first names for men:

Jack    Tom    Dick    Harry

Do you know any others?

## PRESENTATION OF THE READING
### Prereading Questions

Have students discuss these questions before they read the story:

1. Do you know any millionaires?
2. Do you know a person who is good at doing many things?

## COMPREHENSION QUESTIONS

Have students answer these questions after they read the story:

1. Is Virgil a man of means? How do you know?
   (Yes. He is a millionaire.)
2. Is Virgil a true friend?
   (Yes, he is. He is the real McCoy.)
3. How do you know that Virgil is a jack of all trades?
   (He can do many different jobs. He can type letters and repair machines.)
4. Does Virgil want to keep up with the Joneses?
   (No, he doesn't. He doesn't have to have a lot of expensive things.)

## Test Your Memory of the Idioms

Have students do this activity:

> How many people were there in the idioms in the story? Write down as many names as you can remember. Then write down as many of the idioms with people as you can.

# FOLLOW-UP

After students have completed the activities in the unit, have them do one or both of these activities:

1. Write sentences like the following on the board. Have students replace the underlined words with the idioms. Check that students use the correct forms.

   a. Ida and Pete went out. They each paid the cost of their own bill.

   b. I don't want to go out with just any person.

   c. Helen's brothers and sisters are tall. It is a quality shared by the members of her family.

   d. Don't be a person who acts as if you know everything. Other people's opinions are not stupid just because you don't agree with them.

   e. Una can do lots of repairs around the house. She's a person who can do many things.

2. Write the idioms on the board with some of the words missing. Have students supply the missing words.

# Unit 6
# Idioms from Animals

## INTRODUCTION

Tell students that they are going to learn idioms with animals. Do these activities:

Name some animals you know in English.

Do you know these animals?

| | | | | | |
|---|---|---|---|---|---|
| bat | mouse | worm | cat | chicken | bird |
| horse | pig | rat | turkey | dog | |

## PRESENTATION OF THE READING
### Prereading Questions

Have students discuss these questions before they read the story:

1. Do you have a brother or a sister? How are you the same or different?
2. Some people like to get up early and do things early. Are you like that or are you a late person?
3. What do you know about football? Do you like the game?

## COMPREHENSION QUESTIONS

Have students answer these questions after they read the story:

1. Does Randy have a brother?
   (Yes. He has a twin brother, Jason.)
2. What was Randy like?
   (Randy was shy and as quiet as a mouse.)
3. Who loved to read?
   (Randy loved to read. He was the bookworm.)
4. Could Randy see well?
   (No. He could not see well. Without glasses, he was as blind as a bat.)
5. Who got out of bed at four every morning?
   (Both Randy and Jason got out of bed at four every morning. Both of them were early birds.)

6. What do each of the brothers do now?

(Jason is quarterback of a football team, and Randy is the owner of the team.)

## Test Your Memory of the Idioms

Have students do this activity:

How many animals were there in the idioms in the story? Write down as many of them as you can remember. Then write down as many of the idioms with animals as you can.

# FOLLOW-UP

After students have completed the activities in the unit, have them do one or both of these activities:

1. There are many idioms in English with animals. Here are some others you might want to introduce to the students. You may want students to look in dictionaries and other reference books to find others to add to the list. Help students to write sentences with the idioms.

to eat like a bird: to eat very little

as a duck takes to water: easily and naturally

like a fish out of water: a person who feels as if he or she is in a foreign environment

to let the cat out of the bag: to tell a secret

to put the cart before the horse: to do something less important before something more important

to make a beeline: to head straight toward something

2. Write down the story from the unit on the board, eliminating the idioms. Have students supply the idioms.

# Unit 7
# Idioms from Geography

## INTRODUCTION

Tell students that they are going to learn idioms from geography. Ask them these questions:

Do you know these words connected with geography? What do they mean?

| | | | |
|---|---|---|---|
| dirt | earth | hill | moon |
| woods | world | iceberg | landslide |

What is a creek? (It's a small narrow mountain stream.)

What is a molehill? (A mole is an animal that lives under the ground. It digs a hole to live in. It makes a little hill of earth above the hole. This is the molehill.)

## PRESENTATION OF THE READING
### Prereading Questions

Have students discuss these questions before they read the story:

1. Do you prefer to live in a small town or a big town? Tell why.
2. Does your town have a mayor? What does the mayor do?

## COMPREHENSION QUESTIONS

Have students answer these questions after they read the story:

1. Do many exciting things happen in the person's town?
   (No. Exciting things happen once in a blue moon.)
2. What kind of town is Bobtown?
   (It's a quiet, sleepy old town.)
3. Why is the town going downhill?
   (Many citizens have moved away. There are many empty houses, and real estate is dirt cheap.)
4. What kind of people live in Bobtown?
   (The people are down-to-earth. They are not afraid to say what they think. They do not make a mountain out of a molehill.)

5. What happens in the elections for mayor?

   (The same person wins by a landslide.)

## Test Your Memory of the Idioms

Have students do this activity:

> How many geography words were there in the idioms in the story? Write down as many of the geography words as you can. Then write down as many of the idioms with geography words as you can.

# FOLLOW-UP

After students have completed the activities in the unit, have them do one or both of these activities:

1. Write the eleven idioms in the unit on the board, eliminating the geography words. Have students supply the geography words.
2. Write the following situations on the board, and have students write sentences to describe the situations:
   a. Yolanda likes to cook. She eats in restaurants very seldom.
   b. We ate at the Chinese restaurant on the corner yesterday. The food was excellent. We plan to eat there again today.
   c. The food in that restaurant is very cheap. I don't see how they serve so much food as such low prices.
   d. Our friend Tara is very popular in school. She is sure to win the election for class president by a large number of votes.
   e. My uncle had a major operation last month, and he was very seriously ill. Now he is home and he feels much better.

# Unit 8
# Idioms from Recreation

## INTRODUCTION

Tell students that they are going to learn idioms that have words from recreation. Do these activities:

Sports and games are kinds of recreation. What kinds of sports and games do you know?

Find the meaning of the following words. Then group the words that belong to the same sport or recreation together. You may use the same word several times, for different sports.

| | | | | |
|---|---|---|---|---|
| ball | bat | dice | cards | base |
| kick | boat | sink | swim | |

## PRESENTATION OF THE READING
### Prereading Questions

Have students discuss these questions before they read the story:

1. Do you know people who are very direct and open? These are people who will tell you what they think.
2. Is it good or bad to be direct?
3. Are Americans in general more direct than the people in your native country?

## COMPREHENSION QUESTIONS

Have students answer these questions after they read the story:

1. What was Winona's style?
   (She was direct and open. She always put her cards on the table right off the bat.)
2. What would she do if you did something wrong?
   (She told you that you were off base.)
3. When she said no, what did she mean?
   (When she said no, she meant no. No dice.)
4. Did many people argue with Winona and win?
   (No. Not many people argued with her and won.)

5. Did she like people who stood up to her and said what they thought? (Yes, she did. She secretly got a kick out of it.)

## Test Your Memory of the Idioms

Have students do this activity:

> How many recreation words were there in the idioms in the story? Write down as many of them as you can remember. Then write down as many of the idioms with words from recreation as you can.

# FOLLOW-UP

After students have completed the activities in the unit, have them do one or both of these activities:

1. On the board, write down the definitions from the Meanings section in the text. Have students write the idiom for each definition.
2. Write sentences like the following on the board. Have students replace the underlined words with the idioms. Check that students use the correct forms.
   a. My boss is <u>very effective and efficient</u>.
   b. I met Lila and we liked each other <u>immediately</u>.
   c. We both <u>have the same problem</u>: we need to earn more money to pay for school.
   d. Both management and employees <u>explained their situation fully and honestly</u>.
   e. I am going to speak only English, <u>no matter what</u>.

# Unit 9
# Idioms with the Word *And*

## INTRODUCTION

Tell students that they are going to learn idioms that have the word **and**. Ask them this question:

Why do you think each pair of words goes together?

wear and tear (sound alike)              song and dance (related activities)

ins and outs (opposites)                 back and forth (opposites)

## PRESENTATION OF THE READING

### Prereading Questions

Have students discuss these questions before they read the story:

1. What kinds of repairs can you do to a car?
2. What do we call a person who repairs cars?
3. When you cannot repair your car, where do you take it?

## COMPREHENSION QUESTIONS

Have students answer these questions after they read the story:

1. Is the person's car old?
   (Yes, it is. It is eleven years old.)
2. Does the person's car have many problems?
   (By and large, the person's car runs okay.)
3. How does the person use the car?
   (The person uses it to go back and forth to work every day.)
4. What do the mechanics know?
   (They know all about the person's car. They know the ins and outs of the person's car.)
5. Do the mechanics give the person a song and dance?
   (No. They tell the person exactly what's wrong and how much it will cost to fix it.)

6. Does the person feel confident when driving the car?
(Yes.)

## Test Your Memory of the Idioms

Have students do this activity:

How many idioms with the word **and** were there in the story? Write down as many of the idioms with the word **and** as you can.

# FOLLOW-UP

After students have completed the activities in the unit, have them do one or both of these activities:

1. Write the eleven pairs of words on the board, with the order of the pairs mixed up. Have students write the idioms in the correct form. Here are some examples:

   dance/song     ends/odds     ins/outs

2. Here are some other idioms with **and** you might want to introduce to the students. You may want students to look in dictionaries and other reference books to find others to add to the list. Help students to write sentences with the idioms.

   right and wrong: what are good or bad ways of acting, no matter what

   bright and early: very early

   nice and easy: very carefully or slowly

   flesh and blood: one's family, relatives

   heart and soul: with all one's feelings

   skin and bones: very thin

# Unit 10
# Idioms from Household Items and Tools

## INTRODUCTION

Tell students that they are going to learn idioms with household items and tools. Ask them this question:

What are each of these household items used for?

| a tack | nails | a hatchet | a pan |
| a screw | pins | needles | a pot |
| soap | a sponge | a blanket | |

## PRESENTATION OF THE READING

### Prereading Questions

Have students discuss these questions before they read the story:

1. Have you ever been onstage? What did you do?
2. Do you like to talk before a large group? How do you feel?
3. What is a ventriloquist? What does a ventriloquist do?

## COMPREHENSION QUESTIONS

Have students answer these questions after they read the story:

1. Who wanted to be in the talent show?

   (Marta)

2. Why did the person agree to be in the talent show?

   (Because Marta said the person was a wet blanket. The person did not want to argue with her.)

3. What kind of act did the person do?

   (The person did a ventriloquist act. It looked as if the person and the puppet were telling jokes.)

4. Did the audience like the act?

   (Yes. The audience laughed and seemed to enjoy the act.)

5. Why was Marta angry?

   (Marta was angry because she did not win the contest and because her friend won.)

6. Have the friends buried the hatchet?

(Yes. They are now friends again.)

7. Has the person continued to go on the stage?

(No. The person has not been on the stage before or since.)

## Test Your Memory of the Idioms

Have students do this activity:

How many household items and tools were there in the idioms in the story? Write down as many of them as you can remember. Then write down as many of the idioms with household items and tools as you can.

## FOLLOW-UP

After students have completed the activities in the unit, have them do one or both of these activities:

1. Write down the eleven idioms in the unit on the board, eliminating the words for household items and tools. Have students supply the missing words.
2. Write sentences like the following on the board. Have students write down the idiom that relates to each situation.

   a. Ryan talks to himself and people think that he is strange.

   b. My friend's child is very smart. She is only two and she can count.

   c. Julie goes out very seldom. When she goes to parties, she just sits in the corner.

   d. I couldn't get my computer program to work. I stopped working on it after two hours.

   e. On the first day of school, I was very nervous waiting for class to start.

# Unit 11
# Idioms from Medicine

## INTRODUCTION

Tell students that they are going to learn idioms with words from medicine. Ask these questions:

What is a pill? When do you take one?
What is a pain?
What is a nerve?
What is ointment? When do you use it?
What color is blood?
What do you do when you get burned?

Have students do these activities:

Hold your breath.
Cough.
Point to your bones.

## PRESENTATION OF THE READING
### Prereading Questions

Have students discuss these questions before they read the story:

1. Do you like birds? What kinds of birds do you like?
2. Why are birds a problem if you have a garden and grow vegetables?
3. What is a scarecrow?

## COMPREHENSION QUESTIONS

Have students answer these questions after they read the story:

1. Does the person usually like birds?
   (Yes. They are beautiful when they fly. Many of them have lovely colors.)
2. Did the person like the bird that came into the back yard?
   (No. The bird caused trouble. It ate all the baby lettuces in the garden.)
3. What did the bird take pains to do?
   (It took pains to eat the best lettuce.)

4. What did the person do to stop the bird and give it a taste of its own medicine? (The person built a scarecrow.)

5. Did the scarecrow scare the bird? How do you know? (No. The bird was pulling out straws from the scarecrow's hat.)

## Test Your Memory of the Idioms

Have students do this activity:

> How many words from medicine were there in the idioms in the story? Write down as many of them as you can. Then write down as many of the idioms with words from medicine as you can.

## FOLLOW-UP

After students have completed the activities in the unit, have them do one or both of these activities:

1. Write the eleven idioms in the unit on the board, eliminating the words from medicine. Have students supply the missing words.

2. On the board, write the definitions from the Meanings section in the text. Have students write the idiom for each definition.

# Unit 12
# Idioms from Plants

## INTRODUCTION

Tell students that they are going to learn idioms with plants. Ask them these questions:

> What is a bush? Is it like a small tree? (yes)
> If a flower is in bud, is it opened or closed? (closed) Is it going to open? (yes)
> What is a nutshell? (the "outside skin" of a nut)
> Do straw and hay look the same? (yes)
> What is a grapevine? (the plant on which grapes grow)

## PRESENTATION OF THE READING

### Prereading Questions

Have students discuss these questions before they read the story:

1. Describe an easy and comfortable life.
2. Can people who never make a decision be successful in life?
3. Can people make big changes in the way they act, or do people never change?

## COMPREHENSION QUESTIONS

Have students answer these questions after they read the story:

1. What did Eustacia want?

   (She wanted everything to be easy and comfortable. She wanted her life to be a bed of roses.)

2. When she had a decision to make, could she make it?

   (No, she couldn't.)

3. When you asked her what she was going to do, what did she do?

   (She beat around the bush. She never gave a direct answer.)

4. Did she decide to change her life?

   (Yes, she did. She decided to turn over a new leaf.)

5. Did she finally change her life? Why?

   (No, she didn't. She could not decide what to do.)

6. How would you describe Eustacia?

(In a nutshell, she is not good at making decisions.)

## Test Your Memory of the Idioms

Have students do this activity:

How many words related to plants were there in the idioms in the story? Write down as many of them as you can remember. Then write down as many of the idioms with plants as you can.

# FOLLOW-UP

After students have completed the activities in the unit, have them do one or both of these activities:

1. Write the eleven idioms in the unit on the board, eliminating the plant words. Have students supply the missing words.
2. Write sentences like the following on the board. Have students write the idiom that relates to each situation.

   a. In an office, people often find out information by talking to other people.

   b. Many people think that life is easy and comfortable for rich people.

   c. I worked ten hours without stopping.

   d. Many things have gone wrong today. Now I can't find my car keys. I just can't take any more.

   e. I want you to briefly tell me about your work experience.

   f. My computer just stopped working, and I need to finish an assignment for tomorrow.

# Unit 13
# Idioms from Clothes

## INTRODUCTION

Tell students that they are going to learn idioms with clothes. Do these activities:

How many clothes names do you know in English? Give the names and write them down.

Do you know these?

cap     gloves     collar     shoestring     apron

## PRESENTATION OF THE READING
### Prereading Questions

Have students discuss these questions before they read the story:

1. Do you get angry easily? Do some people get angry more easily than others?
2. Would you prefer to be an employee or the boss? Tell why.

## COMPREHENSION QUESTIONS

Have students answer these questions after they read the story:

1. Who gets angry easily?
   (The person's boss gets angry easily.)
2. Is the boss always angry?
   (Yes. He is always hot under the collar about something.)
3. What does the boss think if sales are bad?
   (He thinks that he is going to lose everything. He thinks he is going to lose his shirt.)
4. Does the business make a lot of money?
   (No, it doesn't. It runs on a shoestring.)
5. Does the person want to be in the boss's place?
   (No. The person doesn't want to be in the boss's shoes.)

## Test Your Memory of the Idioms

Have students do this activity:

How many kinds of clothes were there in the idioms in the story? Write down as many of them as you can remember. Then write down as many of the idioms with clothes as you can.

# FOLLOW-UP

After students have completed the activities in the unit, have them do one or both of these activities:

1. On the board, write the definitions from the Meanings section in the text. Have students write the idiom for each definition.
2. Here are some other idioms with clothes you might want to introduce to the students. You may want students to look in dictionaries and other reference books to find others to add to the list. Help students to write sentences with the idioms.

   at the drop of a hat: immediately

   to be old hat: to be out of date

   to wear more than one hat: to do more than one job

   well-heeled: with a lot of money

   to have the shoe on the other foot: to experience a completely different situation (from the previous situation)

   fall apart at the seams: to break into pieces, to totally fail

   by the seat of one's pants: by luck, without much knowledge or skill

# Unit 14
# Idioms from Time

## INTRODUCTION

Tell students that they are going to learn idioms with time. Present this activity:

Each country or culture has its own rules about time: what is late, what is early, what is on time. What do you think of this story?

Liz has invited some friends to dinner at her house at eight tonight. It is now eight fifteen. Liz is upset because nobody has arrived and the dinner is ready. She wonders if anybody will come or if maybe something bad has happened. Why is Liz thinking this way? Would you think that way?

## PRESENTATION OF THE READING

### Prereading Questions

Have students discuss these questions before they read the story:

1. How do cats spend their time?
2. Are cats good pets? Tell why.
3. Do cats sometimes get stuck in trees and can't come down? Have you ever seen a cat that was stuck someplace?

## COMPREHENSION QUESTIONS

Have students answer these questions after they read the story:

1. Is the cat good at waiting for things to happen?
   (Yes. Waiting and killing time is her specialty.)
2. Does she usually make plans?
   (No, she doesn't. She usually does things on the spur of the moment.)
3. When does she go fishing?
   (She goes fishing when she feels the time is right.)
4. What is the cat's favorite hobby?
   (Her favorite hobby is tree climbing.)
5. What comes to help get the cat down?
   (The fire truck comes to help get the cat down.)

6. What does the cat do when she hears the fire truck?

(The cat jumps out of the tree.)

7. How does the cat land?

(The cat lands on all four feet.)

## Test Your Memory of the Idioms

Have students do this activity:

How many idioms with time were there in the story? Write down as many of the idioms with time as you can.

## FOLLOW-UP

After students have completed the activities in the unit, have them do one or both of these activities:

1. On the board, write the definitions from the Meanings section in the text. Have students write the idiom for each definition.

2. Write the story from the unit on the board, eliminating the idioms. Have students supply the idioms.

# Unit 15
# Idioms from the Weather

## INTRODUCTION

Tell students that they are going to learn idioms from the weather. Ask them these questions:

Do you know these words or expressions related to the weather? What do they mean?

| | | | |
|---|---|---|---|
| fair | weather | clouds | storm |
| snow | ice | rainy | day |

What kind of wind is a breeze? (a light wind)

## PRESENTATION OF THE READING

### Prereading Questions

Have students discuss these questions before they read the story:

1. Do you think that some people are lucky all the time?
2. Do you know some people who are lucky all the time? What good things happen to them?

## COMPREHENSION QUESTIONS

Have students answer these questions after they read the story:

1. Is life easy for some people?

   (Yes. For some people, everything is easy. Life is a breeze.)

2. Are some people always healthy?

   (Yes. They are always healthy. They are never under the weather.)

3. When these people walk into a room full of strangers, do they make friends easily?

   (Yes, they do. They have no trouble breaking the ice.)

4. What do they earn enough to do?

   (They earn enough to save some money every week. They are saving money for a rainy day.)

5. Do some people have no problems if times are good or bad?

(Yes. They are okay come rain or shine.)

## Test Your Memory of the Idioms

Have students do this activity:

How many words about weather were there in the idioms in the story? Write as many weather words as you can remember. Then write as many of the idioms from the weather as you can.

# FOLLOW-UP

After students have completed the activities in the unit, have them do one or both of these activities:

1. Write the story from the unit on the board, eliminating the idioms. Have students supply the idioms.
2. Write sentences like the following on the board. Have students replace the underlined words with the idioms. Check that students use the correct forms.
   a. It <u>was raining very hard</u> when I was walking home.
   b. Albert is a true friend. He is not <u>a person who doesn't help a friend who needs help</u>.
   c. Learning languages is <u>something very easy</u> for Paul.
   d. I'll be at the meeting, <u>no matter how hard it is to do</u>.
   e. I didn't go to the game because I was <u>sick</u>.
   f. I didn't go to the game because I was <u>busy with a lot of work that I had to do</u>.

# Unit 16
# Idioms from around the House

## INTRODUCTION

Tell students that they are going to learn idioms with words from around the house. Ask them these questions:

What words do you know that are related to the house?

Do you know these words that are related to the house? What do they mean?

| | | | |
|---|---|---|---|
| drain | wall | door | ceiling |
| fence | shelf | steps | table |

## PRESENTATION OF THE READING

### Prereading Questions

Have students discuss these questions before they read the story:

1. Do you like to listen to jokes?
2. What do comedians do? Do you know the names of any comedians? Do you know any of their jokes?
3. Is it easy to become a comedian?

## COMPREHENSION QUESTIONS

Have students answer these questions after they read the story:

1. What happened when Ron told his father that he wanted to be a comedian?
   (His father hit the ceiling and shouted.)
2. Did Ron's father think that Ron would be a success?
   (No. Ron's father thought that Ron was throwing his college education down the drain and that Ron would be a bum.)
3. What steps did Ron take to become a good comedian?
   (He studied acting, talked to comedians, and kept a book of jokes.)
4. Was Ron's comedy act successful?
   (Yes. Soon his act was bringing down the house.)
5. What happened when Ron returned to the town?
   (The town gave him a big welcome. The town rolled out the red carpet. There was a big parade.)

## Test Your Memory of the Idioms

Have students do this activity:

> How many words related to the house were there in the idioms in the story? Write as many as you can remember. Then write as many of the idioms with words from around the house as you can.

## FOLLOW-UP

After students have completed the activities in the unit, have them do one or both of these activities:

1. Write the eleven idioms in the unit on the board, eliminating the words from around the house. Have students supply the missing words.

2. Write sentences like the following on the board. Have students write the idiom that relates to each situation.

    a. We often go to that restaurant because the soup is free.

    b. Work was always very important to Robert. Now he is retired and he feels very useless. He doesn't know what to do with his time.

    c. We are uncertain about what we should do. Should we buy a station wagon or a jeep?

    d. My husband doesn't put the cover back on the toothpaste tube. I can't stand this any longer.

    e. Here is a typical American success story: a person starts work in the mail room and becomes president of the company. All you need to do is to get that first job to get a chance to succeed.

# Unit 17
# Idioms with the Word *As*

## INTRODUCTION

Tell students that they are going to learn idioms with the word **as.** Do these activities:

In English, as in many other languages, we make comparisons. One way to make comparisons is to use **as . . . as.**

One common comparison is to compare people with animals. Some of the comparisons in this unit compare people to animals. Sometimes it is difficult to understand why we compare people to certain animals. For example, in English we say "as sick as a dog." Are dogs always sick? Does the comparison seem good?

Discuss some of the other animals in the unit. Let students tell what they know about the animals. Prompt as necessary.

Let's look at some other animals you will study in this unit. What kind of animal is a mule? What special characteristics does it have? (stubborn)

What is a kitten? What is special about a kitten? Do you think kittens are weak? What kind of animal is a lark? (A bird. A lark is known for its beautiful song.) What is characteristic of a bee? (They are always busy looking for food.) What is characteristic of a bear?

## PRESENTATION OF THE READING

### Prereading Questions

Have students discuss these questions before they read the story:

1. How do you feel when you have the flu?
2. How long does it take to get over the flu and feel better?

## COMPREHENSION QUESTIONS

Have students answer these questions after they read the story:

1. What was wrong with the person last week?
   (The person had the flu. The person was as sick as a dog.)
2. How did the person feel?
   (The person felt as weak as a kitten.)

3. How often did Clarence call?

(Clarence called every morning and evening. His calls were as regular as clockwork.)

4. Did the fever go away immediately?

(No, it did not go away immediately. It was as stubborn as a mule.)

5. What happened on day five?

(The person felt as hungry as a bear.)

6. How does the person feel now?

(The person is fine. The person feels as fit as a fiddle.)

## Test Your Memory of the Idioms

Have students do this activity:

How many idioms with **as** were there in the story? Write down as many of the idioms with **as** as you can.

## FOLLOW-UP

After students have completed the activities in the unit, have them do one or both of these activities:

1. Write the adjectives from the idioms in one column on the board (**sick, stubborn,** and so on) and the nouns in a second column (**bear, dog,** and so on). Have students match the two columns.

2. Here are some other idioms with **as** you might want to introduce to the students. You may want students to look in dictionaries and other reference books to find others to add to the list. Help students to write sentences with the idioms. Note that all these idioms add the meaning of "very" to the adjective.

as black as midnight: very dark

as clear as a bell: very clear (used of voices)

as plain as the nose on your face: very obvious and easy to see

as light as a feather: very light, not heavy at all

as quick as lightning: very fast at figuring things out

as smooth as velvet: very soft to the touch

as tough as leather: very hard to cut or chew (as of meat)

# Unit 18
# Idioms with Repetition

## INTRODUCTION

Tell students that they are going to learn idioms with repetition. Present this:

The idioms we are going to study have sounds that are repeated. What do these idioms have in common?

humdrum    wishy-washy    mumbo jumbo    fuddy-duddy

(The last two or three sounds are repeated.)

Tell students:
Look for the repeated sounds as we study the idioms in this unit.

## PRESENTATION OF THE READING

### Prereading Questions

Have students discuss these questions before they read the story:

1. Do you know a person who is a character? This means a person who acts very differently from other people.
2. Do you like people who are characters?

## COMPREHENSION QUESTIONS

Have students answer these questions after they read the story:

1. What did people think of Uncle Max?

   (They thought he was crazy.)
2. What was his office like?

   (It was topsy-turvy. There were papers all over.)
3. What was Max always trying to explain?

   (He was always trying to explain some scientific mumbo jumbo. No one could understand it.)
4. What did people discover later?

   (They discovered that Max was a very important scientist.)
5. Why didn't people know what Max did?

   (Max worked in a secret government operation. He worked on hush-hush projects.)

6. What kind of scientist was he?

(He was a hotshot rocket technician.)

## Test Your Memory of the Idioms

Have students do this activity:

How many idioms with repetition were there in the story? Write as many of the idioms with repetition as you can.

# FOLLOW-UP

After students have completed the activities in the unit, have them do one or both of these activities:

1. On the board, write the definitions from the Meanings section in the text. Have students write the idioms for each definition.
2. Write sentences like the following on the board. Have students write the idiom that relates to each situation.
   a. I like to take my time getting ready in the morning. I don't like to rush. But sometimes I am late for school.
   b. In bed, I could hear the sound of the steady rain on the window.
   c. My life is so boring. I do the same thing every day.
   d. The burglars scattered things all over the house. The house was a mess when the owners returned.
   e. If you need someone to fix your car, ask Pedro. He's very good at doing repairs—and he lets you know that he is good at it.

# Unit 19
# Idioms with Words That Go Together I

## INTRODUCTION

Tell students this:

> In this unit, you are going to learn some words that go together and that have special meanings. These words are idioms like the ones we have studied so far in the book. You will notice that people use the idioms that we are going to study often in talking. Here are some examples:
>
> more or less    the other day    every other
>
> Have you ever heard any of these idioms? Do you know what they mean?

## PRESENTATION OF THE READING

### Prereading Questions

Have students discuss these questions before they read the story:

1. What kinds of games do you like to play? Do you like video games? Are you good at games?
2. What is a jigsaw puzzle?
3. Have you ever put together a jigsaw puzzle?

## COMPREHENSION QUESTIONS

Have students answer these questions after they read the story:

1. What did the person decide to do?
   (The person decided to put together a 5,000-piece jigsaw puzzle.)
2. Is the person good at games?
   (Yes. The person is good at all kinds of games, from crossword puzzles to video games.)
3. Was doing the puzzle easy after all?
   (No. Doing the puzzle wasn't so easy after all.)
4. How long did the person stare at the puzzle?
   (The person stared at the puzzle for two hours.)

5. How long did it take the person to finish the puzzle?

   (It took the person quite a few months.)

6. When did the person find the missing piece? Where?

   (The person found the missing piece just the other day. The piece was behind the sofa.)

## Test Your Memory of the Idioms

Have students do this activity:

How many idioms with words that go together were there in the story? Write down as many of the idioms with words that go together as you can.

## FOLLOW-UP

After students have completed the activities in the unit, have them do one or both of these activities:

1. On the board, write the definitions from the Meanings section in the text. Have students write the idiom for each definition.

2. Write sentences like the following on the board. Have students replace the underlined words with the idioms. Check that students use the correct forms.

   a. I bought a car <u>recently</u>.

   b. <u>Many</u> students were late for class today because of the bad traffic.

   c. I will learn to speak English well <u>eventually</u>.

   d. I make supper <u>one day but not the next</u>.

   e. You are working too hard. You need to <u>relax</u>.

# Unit 20
# Idioms with Words That Go Together II

## INTRODUCTION

Tell students this:

> In this unit, you are going to learn more English idioms with words that go together and that have special meanings. You studied some in unit 19. Here are some examples of idioms you are going to study in this unit:
>
> once in a while    as a matter of fact    to take turns
>
> Have you ever heard any of these idioms? Do you know what they mean?

## PRESENTATION OF THE READING

### Prereading Questions

Have students discuss these questions before they read the story:

1. Have you ever had something lucky happen to you? What happened?
2. Why do you think that buying lottery tickets is popular with people? Do you think it is a good idea to buy lottery tickets?
3. What would you do if you won the lottery?

## COMPREHENSION QUESTIONS

Have students answer these questions after they read the story:

1. What do the person and the brother buy each week?
   (They buy one lottery ticket.)
2. Does the person buy a lottery ticket every week?
   (No. The person and the brother take turns. One week the person buys the ticket. The next week the brother buys the ticket.)
3. What was different one week? What happened for a change?
   (The brother's girlfriend bought the ticket.)
4. What happened that week?
   (They won the lottery. They won $46 million and 7 cents.)
5. Who shared the money?
   (The person, the brother, and the girlfriend shared the money.)

## Test Your Memory of the Idioms

Have students do this activity:

> How many idioms with words that go together were there in the story? Write down as many of the idioms with words that go together as you can.

# FOLLOW-UP

After students have completed the activities in the unit, have them do one or both of these activities:

1. On the board, write the definitions from the Meanings section in the text. Have students write the idiom for each definition.
2. Write sentences like the following on the board. Have students replace the underlined words with the idioms. Check that students use the correct forms.

   a. To do something different, let's take a walk and not watch TV.
   b. I am not very busy. In truth, I have nothing to do.
   c. Mostly but not always, I can understand what the professor says.
   d. I didn't forget to buy you a present for your birthday by plan.
   e. Olive has a lot of money. Although this is true, she doesn't like to spend a penny.

# Answer Key

## UNIT 1
## IDIOMS FROM COLORS
### Meanings

1. out of the blue
2. in black and white
3. in the red
4. red tape
5. the green light
6. the red carpet
7. the black market
8. a white lie
9. green with envy
10. to feel blue
11. in the black

### Practice

A.

1. no
2. no
3. yes
4. yes
5. no
6. no
7. yes
8. yes
9. yes
10. no
11. yes

B.

1. I got the news out of the blue.
2. The rules for the contest were in black and white.
3. They were green with envy when their friend won the lottery.
4. Tony loves to shop, so he is always in the red.
5. You must go through a lot of red tape to get a visa in some countries.
6. They rolled out the red carpet when he came.
7. Yuri does not have a problem with money. He's in the black.
8. Pam was feeling blue because she had to stay at home.
9. I told a white lie. I said I couldn't come to the party because I had other plans.
10. The city has the green light to build a new highway.
11. The tourists bought some money on the black market.

# UNIT 2
# IDIOMS FROM FOOD
## Meanings

1. in a pickle
2. a piece of cake
3. a lemon
4. to cream someone
5. peanuts
6. baloney
7. fishy
8. to go bananas
9. nuts
10. a peach
11. the apple of one's eye

## Practice

A.

1. no
2. yes
3. yes
4. no
5. yes

6. yes

7. no

8. yes

9. no

10. yes

11. yes

B.

1. Using the computer was so easy, it was a piece of cake.

2. Something fishy must be happening. We're the only ones here, but I'm hearing strange noises.

3. That man doesn't know anything, but he talks as if he knows everything. Everything he says is baloney.

4. My new TV is a lemon. It has a very bad picture.

5. Millie was in a pickle when the police officer stopped her for speeding.

6. The dog went nuts when its owner came home.

7. In the soccer tournament, our team creamed its opponent 8 to 1.

8. The team went bananas when it won the championship.

9. Norma is very nice. She's a peach.

10. Jason bought a used stereo for peanuts, and it sounds really good.

11. I'm the apple of my grandmother's eye.

# UNIT 3
# IDIOMS FROM NUMBERS

## Meanings

1. forty winks

2. on second thought

3. in seventh heaven, on cloud nine

4. sixth sense

5. second nature

6. six of one, half a dozen of the other

7. of two minds

8. to put two and two together

9. second to none

10. at first sight

## Practice

A.

1. yes
2. no
3. yes
4. no
5. no
6. yes
7. yes
8. no
9. yes
10. yes
11. yes

B.

1. At first sight
2. second nature
3. second to none
4. of two minds
5. On second thought
6. put two and two together
7. in seventh heaven, on cloud nine
8. forty winks
9. sixth sense
10. six of one, half a dozen of the other

# UNIT 4
# IDIOMS FROM PARTS OF THE BODY

## Meanings

1. to have a sweet tooth
2. nosey
3. a big mouth
4. see eye to eye

5. a long face
6. by heart
7. to shake a leg
8. to cost an arm and a leg
9. head over heels in love
10. to pull someone's leg
11. a pain in the neck

## Practice

A.

1. no
2. no
3. yes
4. no
5. yes
6. yes
7. no
8. yes
9. yes
10. yes
11. yes

B.

1. George really had a long face because he had lost his wallet.
2. Our neighbors are nosey.
3. She loves cakes. She has such a sweet tooth.
4. They never see eye to eye.
5. That person has a big mouth.
6. Come on! Shake a leg!
7. Lisa is head over heels in love with Steve.
8. Driving in this terrible traffic is a pain in the neck.
9. Don't believe her. She's pulling your leg.
10. I learned that poem by heart.
11. That excellent stereo system must cost an arm and a leg.

# UNIT 5
# IDIOMS FROM PEOPLE
## Meanings

1. the real McCoy
2. to keep up with the Joneses
3. a jack of all trades
4. a man/woman of means
5. to go Dutch
6. a smart aleck, a wise guy
7. Tom, Dick, or Harry
8. a man/girl Friday
9. to run in the family

## Practice

A.

1. yes
2. no
3. no
4. no
5. no
6. no
7. yes
8. yes
9. no
10. yes

B.

1. This ring is the real McCoy. It's genuine.
2. Bart is broke because he wants to keep up with the Joneses.
3. The president of our company is a woman of means.
4. What we need in this office is a girl Friday.
5. Be careful with Ben. He's somewhat of a wise guy.
6. Being good at math runs in my family.

7. I don't like to work with her. She's such a smart aleck.

8. I don't lend my car to just any Tom, Dick, or Harry.

9. At last I found Andy the handyman. He's a jack of all trades.

10. Amanda asked Richard to go on a date, but she said that they would go Dutch.

# UNIT 6
# IDIOMS FROM ANIMALS
## Meanings

1. as quiet as a mouse
2. to work like a dog
3. pigheaded
4. to eat like a horse
5. an early bird
6. as blind as a bat
7. a bookworm
8. chicken
9. to talk turkey
10. to smell a rat
11. a copycat

## Practice

A.

1. no
2. no
3. no
4. yes
5. yes
6. yes
7. no
8. yes
9. no
10. no
11. no

B.

1. works like a dog
2. early bird(s)
3. as quiet as a mouse
4. copycat
5. eats like a horse
6. smell a rat
7. talk turkey
8. bookworm
9. chicken
10. pigheaded
11. blind as a bat

# UNIT 7
# IDIOMS FROM GEOGRAPHY

## Meanings

1. once in a blue moon
2. over the hill
3. win by a landslide
4. down-to-earth
5. dirt cheap
6. out of the woods
7. out of this world
8. the tip of the iceberg
9. to make a mountain out of a molehill
10. up the creek
11. to go downhill

## Practice

A.

1. yes
2. yes
3. no
4. yes

5. yes

6. yes

7. no

8. no

9. yes

10. yes

11. yes

B.

1. to

2. out of

3. the, of the

4. a, out of a

5. by a

6. in a

7. out of the

8. to go

9. dirt

10. up the

11. hill

# UNIT 8
# IDIOMS FROM RECREATION

## Meanings

1. on the ball

2. right off the bat

3. to get a kick out of something

4. no dice

5. a good sport

6. to put one's cards on the table

7. off base

8. in the same boat

9. to keep the ball rolling

10. to go fly a kite

11. sink or swim

## Practice

A.

1. yes
2. no
3. no
4. yes
5. yes
6. no
7. no
8. no
9. yes
10. yes
11. yes

B.

1. sink or swim
2. good sport
3. on the ball
4. no dice
5. go fly a kite
6. in the same boat
7. keep the ball rolling
8. get a kick out of
9. right off the bat
10. off base
11. putting my cards on the table

## UNIT 9
## IDIOMS WITH THE WORD *AND*

### Meanings

1. wear and tear
2. by and large
3. ins and outs
4. odds and ends

5. safe and sound
6. a song and dance
7. a cock-and-bull story
8. spick-and-span
9. back and forth
10. fair and square
11. right and left

## Practice

A.

1. yes
2. no
3. yes
4. no
5. yes
6. yes
7. no
8. yes
9. no
10. yes
11. yes

B.

1. By and large, people put salt on their food.
2. With the odds and ends she found in the garage, she made a chair.
3. No one likes to play with Peter because he doesn't play fair and square.
4. The kitchen was spick-and-span.
5. He always tells cock-and-bull stories.
6. She'll give you a song and dance as usual.
7. He goes from his bedroom to the kitchen, back and forth every morning, when he's getting ready for work.
8. I was really worried, but then they arrived safe and sound.
9. Ask Sandra. She knows all the ins and outs.
10. These shoes can take a lot of wear and tear.
11. There were reporters all around the movie star. They were asking her questions right and left.

## UNIT 10
## IDIOMS FROM HOUSEHOLD ITEMS AND TOOLS
### Meanings

1. a wet blanket
2. to have a screw loose
3. a flash in the pan
4. as sharp as a tack
5. to bury the hatchet
6. to pan out
7. to sponge off
8. potluck
9. to throw in the towel
10. soap opera
11. on pins and needles

### Practice

A.

1. yes
2. no
3. no
4. yes
5. yes
6. no
7. no
8. yes
9. no
10. yes
11. no

B.

1. off
2. a wet
3. pan out
4. a, loose
5. soap

6. pins, needles
7. the towel
8. in the
9. bury the
10. as a tack
11. potluck

## UNIT 11
## IDIOMS FROM MEDICINE
### Meanings

1. sick and tired
2. blood is thicker than water
3. to have a lot of nerve
4. to take pains
5. to give someone a taste of his/her own medicine
6. to feel something in one's bones
7. to hold one's breath
8. a bitter pill to swallow
9. to cough up
10. to get burned
11. a fly in the ointment

### Practice

A.

1. no
2. yes
3. yes
4. no
5. yes
6. no
7. yes
8. yes
9. yes
10. yes
11. yes

B.

1. fly in the ointment
2. had a lot of nerve
3. takes pains
4. feel it in my bones
5. sick and tired
6. blood is thicker than water
7. got a taste of his own medicine
8. bitter pill to swallow
9. hold your breath
10. get burned
11. cough up

# UNIT 12
# IDIOMS FROM PLANTS

## Meanings

1. a bed of roses
2. to beat around the bush
3. to bark up the wrong tree
4. to turn over a new leaf
5. the last straw
6. in a nutshell
7. to nip something in the bud
8. through the grapevine
9. up a tree
10. to hit the hay
11. bushed

## Practice

A.

1. no
2. yes
3. no
4. no

5. no

6. no

7. no

8. yes

9. no

10. yes

11. yes

B.

1. We had no time to lose, so they told us in a nutshell.

2. If you think she'll help us, you're barking up the wrong tree.

3. Andrew forgot his keys for the third day in a row. It was the last straw for Andrew.

4. Ken had a terrible problem. He was up a tree.

5. Elizabeth's family was very rich. She didn't have to work. Life was a bed of roses for her.

6. After working for twelve hours today to finish the job, Todd was bushed.

7. Let's not beat around the bush. Let's decide right now.

8. After Bud got a new job, he turned over a new leaf.

9. We have to nip this problem in the bud by making a statement to the public.

10. Joan was very tired, so she hit the hay at eight o'clock last night.

11. We heard through the grapevine that we're getting new computers in our office.

# UNIT 13
# IDIOMS FROM CLOTHES

## Meanings

1. hot under the collar

2. on a shoestring

3. to keep one's shirt on

4. to handle someone with kid gloves

5. to lose one's shirt

6. to be in someone else's shoes

7. dressed to kill

8. tied to someone's apron strings

9. a stuffed shirt

10. a feather in one's cap
11. to keep something under one's hat

## Practice

A.

1. no
2. yes
3. yes
4. no
5. yes
6. no
7. no
8. no
9. no
10. no
11. no

B.

1. stuffed shirt
2. feather in your cap
3. lost his shirt
4. in someone else's shoes
5. hot under the collar
6. tied, apron strings
7. on a shoestring
8. keep it under her hat
9. Keep your shirt on
10. dressed to kill
11. handle her with kid gloves

# UNIT 14
# IDIOMS FROM TIME
## Meanings

1. to kill time
2. in no time
3. on the spur of the moment
4. the time is right
5. in the nick of time
6. to take one's time
7. to make time
8. high time
9. the big time
10. to call it a day
11. for the time being

## Practice

A.

1. no
2. yes
3. no
4. yes
5. yes
6. no
7. yes
8. no
9. yes
10. yes
11. yes

B.

1. It's high time he got himself a job.
2. I think we've done a lot of work. Let's call it a day.
3. We're staying at my sister's house for the time being.
4. The police came in no time.
5. We watched TV to kill time while we waited for the cab.

6. That singer is in the big time now.
7. Robin made time to check over my composition.
8. We went to the movies on the spur of the moment.
9. He came with the money in the nick of time.
10. The time is right to buy a house.
11. I like to take my time in the morning and not hurry off to work.

# UNIT 15
# IDIOMS FROM THE WEATHER
## Meanings

1. a breeze
2. under the weather
3. to break the ice
4. come rain or shine
5. to save something for a rainy day
6. to weather the storm
7. full of hot air
8. to have one's head in the clouds
9. to rain cats and dogs
10. snowed under
11. a fair-weather friend

## Practice

A.

1. yes
2. no
3. yes
4. yes
5. yes
6. no
7. no
8. yes
9. yes
10. yes
11. yes

B.

1. the
2. cats, dogs
3. under
4. in the
5. or
6. under the
7. a, day
8. a
9. the storm
10. of, air
11. fair

# UNIT 16
# IDIOMS FROM AROUND THE HOUSE

## Meanings

1. on the house
2. to hit home
3. to hit the ceiling
4. down the drain
5. to drive someone up the wall
6. on the fence
7. to take steps
8. under the table
9. on the shelf
10. to get one's foot in the door
11. to bring down the house

## Practice

A.

1. yes
2. yes
3. no
4. yes

5. no

6. yes

7. yes

8. yes

9. no

10. yes

11. yes

B.

1. The coffee was on the house.

2. Her words about the importance of education hit home.

3. All that money went down the drain.

4. That dripping faucet is driving me up the wall.

5. Kate got her feet in the door as a secretary, and now she is a manager in the company.

6. Aunt Margie thinks she's been left on the shelf.

7. The pop singer was so good, she brought down the house.

8. When my boss heard the news, he hit the ceiling.

9. The school took steps to prevent a fire hazard.

10. The mayor received some money under the table.

11. Sofia was on the fence. She couldn't decide whether to take the job.

# UNIT 17
# IDIOMS WITH THE WORD *AS*

## Meanings

1. as stubborn as a mule

2. as fit as a fiddle

3. as hungry as a bear

4. as weak as a kitten

5. as sick as a dog

6. as regular as clockwork

7. as good as gold

8. as busy as a bee

9. as plain as day
10. as hard as nails
11. as happy as a lark

## Practice

A.

1. yes
2. yes
3. no
4. no
5. yes
6. yes
7. yes
8. no
9. no
10. yes
11. yes

B.

1. My sister Katie is as stubborn as a mule. You can never change her mind.
2. I started to jog and exercise every day, and now I'm as fit as a fiddle.
3. It's as plain as day he needs to wear glasses.
4. My brother always comes home as hungry as a bear.
5. My mother is always as busy as a bee in the house.
6. I get to work at eight every morning as regular as clockwork.
7. The baby-sitter said little Timmy was as good as gold.
8. Don was as sick as a dog yesterday.
9. It's good to see her as happy as a lark.
10. Berta is as hard as nails. She's very strict.
11. After the operation, I felt as weak as a kitten.

## UNIT 18
## IDIOMS WITH REPETITION
### Meanings

1. hush-hush
2. hotshot
3. wishy-washy
4. to dillydally
5. humdrum
6. topsy-turvy
7. tip-top
8. wheeler-dealer
9. mumbo jumbo
10. pitter-patter
11. fuddy-duddy

### Practice

A.

1. no
2. no
3. yes
4. no
5. yes
6. no
7. yes
8. no
9. no
10. no
11. yes

B.

1. hush-hush
2. mumbo jumbo
3. hotshot
4. topsy-turvy
5. tip-top

6. pitter-patter
7. wishy-washy
8. dillydally
9. wheeler-dealer
10. fuddy-duddy
11. humdrum

## UNIT 19
## IDIOMS WITH WORDS THAT GO TOGETHER I
### Meanings

1. the other day
2. more or less
3. every other
4. quite a few
5. never mind
6. before long, sooner or later
7. take it easy
8. above all
9. after all
10. no wonder

### Practice

A.

1. yes
2. no
3. yes
4. yes
5. yes
6. no
7. no
8. yes
9. yes
10. no
11. yes

B.

1. There are quite a few tornadoes in our state each year.

2. Guess who I saw the other day.

3. Look at the dark sky. I think it's going to rain after all.

4. Take it easy. This exercise is fun. Don't work so hard.

5. I'm more or less sure they'll vote for us.

6. Never mind, dad; I can fix the car.

7. Above all, remember to be polite when you meet them.

8. You go skiing and sooner or later you fall down.

9. No wonder you feel sick. You ate too much.

10. Try our banana-chocolate-raisin-nut ice cream sundae, and before long you'll want another one!

11. We worked as a pair on the idioms exercise. Each of us did every other example.


# UNIT 20
# IDIOMS WITH WORDS THAT GO TOGETHER II

## Meanings

1. once in a while

2. as a matter of fact, in fact

3. to take turns

4. for a change

5. might as well

6. even so

7. for a start

8. all of a sudden

9. on the whole

10. on purpose


## Practice

A.

1. yes

2. no

3. yes

4. no

5. no

6. yes

7. yes

8. no

9. yes

10. yes

11. yes

B.

1. All of a sudden it started to rain.

2. Arthur hurt his ankle as he was playing tennis. Even so, that didn't stop him from winning the game.

3. I took a different route to school today for a change.

4. We left the lights on in the house on purpose.

5. He's very tall. In fact, he is six feet, five inches.

6. It's getting late, and so we might as well go home.

7. We take turns doing the laundry.

8. There are a few things wrong with my new apartment. But, on the whole, I like it.

9. As a matter of fact, it took three hours and twenty-one minutes to get here.

10. We usually watch television. Once in a while we go to the movies.

11. Terry needs to get better grades. For a start, he should spend less time watching TV and more time studying.

## REVIEW FOR UNITS 1–3

| | | |
|---|---|---|
| 1. a | 5. c | 9. b |
| 2. a | 6. a | 10. b |
| 3. b | 7. b | 11. c |
| 4. b | 8. c | 12. a |

## REVIEW FOR UNITS 4–6

| | | |
|---|---|---|
| 1. c | 5. b | 9. c |
| 2. b | 6. a | 10. c |
| 3. a | 7. a | 11. a |
| 4. a | 8. b | 12. b |

## REVIEW FOR UNITS 7–9

| | | |
|---|---|---|
| 1. a | 5. b | 9. b |
| 2. c | 6. a | 10. b |
| 3. b | 7. c | 11. a |
| 4. b | 8. a | 12. c |

## REVIEW FOR UNITS 10–12

| | | |
|---|---|---|
| 1. c | 5. b | 9. a |
| 2. a | 6. c | 10. a |
| 3. b | 7. c | 11. c |
| 4. c | 8. c | 12. b |

## REVIEW FOR UNITS 13–15

| | | |
|---|---|---|
| 1. c | 5. a | 9. c |
| 2. b | 6. a | 10. b |
| 3. b | 7. c | 11. a |
| 4. c | 8. a | 12. b |

## REVIEW FOR UNITS 16–18

| | | |
|---|---|---|
| 1. a | 5. a | 9. c |
| 2. b | 6. c | 10. b |
| 3. b | 7. c | 11. a |
| 4. c | 8. b | 12. c |

## REVIEW FOR UNITS 19–20

| | |
|---|---|
| 1. c | 5. b |
| 2. b | 6. a |
| 3. a | 7. c |
| 4. c | 8. b |

# NTC ESL/EFL TEXTS AND MATERIAL
### Junior High—Adult Education

**Computer Software**
Amigo
Basic Vocabulary Builder on Computer

**Language and Culture Readers**
Beginner's English Reader
Advanced Beginner's English Reader
Cultural Encounters in the U.S.A.
Passport to America Series
  California Discovery
  Adventures in the Southwest
  The Coast-to-Coast Mystery
  The New York Connection
Discover America Series
  California, Chicago, Florida, Hawaii,
  New England, New York, Texas,
  Washington, D.C.
Looking at America Series
  Looking at American Signs, Looking at
  American Food, Looking at American
  Recreation, Looking at American Holidays
Time: We the People
Communicative American English
English á la Cartoon

**Text/Audiocassette Learning Packages**
Speak Up! Sing Out!
Listen and Say It Right in English!

**Transparencies**
Everyday Situations in English

**Duplicating Masters and
Black-line Masters**
The Complete ESL/EFL Cooperative and
  Communicative Activity Book
Easy Vocabulary Games
Vocabulary Games
Advanced Vocabulary Games
Play and Practice!
Basic Vocabulary Builder
Practical Vocabulary Builder
Beginning Activities for English
  Language Learners
Intermediate Activities for English
  Language Learners
Advanced Activities for English
  Language Learners

**Language-Skills Texts**
Starting English with a Smile
English with a Smile
More English with a Smile
English Survival Series
  Building Vocabulary, Recognizing Details,
  Identifying Main Ideas, Writing Sentences
  and Paragraphs, Using the Context
English Across the Curriculum
Essentials of Reading and Writing English
Everyday English
Everyday Situations for Communicating in
  English
Learning to Listen in English
Listening to Communicate in English
Communication Skillbooks
Living in the U.S.A.
Basic English Vocabulary Builder Activity Book
Basic Everyday Spelling Workbook
Practical Everyday Spelling Workbook

Advanced Readings and Communicative
  Activities for Oral Proficiency
Practical English Writing Skills
Express Yourself in Written English
Campus English
English Communication Skills for Professionals
Speak English!
Read English!
Write English!
Orientation in American English
Building English Sentences
Grammar for Use
Grammar Step-by-Step
Listening by Doing
Reading by Doing
Speaking by Doing
Vocabulary by Doing
Writing by Doing
Look, Think and Write

**Life- and Work-Skills Texts**
English for Success
Building Real Life English Skills
Everyday Consumer English
Book of Forms
Essential Life Skills series
Finding a Job in the United States
English for Adult Living
Living in English
Prevocational English

**TOEFL and University Preparation**
NTC's Preparation Course for the TOEFL®
NTC's Practice Tests for the TOEFL®
How to Apply to American Colleges
  and Universities
The International Student's Guide
  to the American University

**Dictionaries and References**
ABC's of Languages and Linguistics
Everyday American English Dictionary
Building Dictionary Skills in
  English (workbook)
Beginner's Dictionary of American
  English Usage
Beginner's English Dictionary
  Workbook
NTC's American Idioms Dictionary
NTC's Dictionary of American Slang
  and Colloquial Expressions
NTC's Dictionary of Phrasal Verbs
NTC's Dictionary of Grammar Terminology
Essential American Idioms
Contemporary American Slang
Forbidden American English
101 American English Idioms
101 American English Proverbs
Practical Idioms
Essentials of English Grammar
The Complete ESL/EFL Resource Book
Safari Grammar
Safari Punctuation
303 Dumb Spelling Mistakes
TESOL Professional Anthologies
  Grammar and Composition
  Listening, Speaking, and Reading
  Culture

For further information or a current catalog, write:
National Textbook Company
a division of *NTC Publishing Group*
4255 West Touhy Avenue
Lincolnwood, Illinois 60646-1975 U.S.A.